Script A - Z

LeeAnne Krusemark
Copyright © 2016 LeeAnne Krusemark

All rights reserved.

ISBN-13: 978-1530809936
ISBN-10: 1530809932

The Complete Glossary of 300+ Terms for all Scriptwriters
(Television, Stage, and Movies)

The following is a listing of more than 300 words and phrases you should be familiar with, so you won't be branded an amateur in the scriptwriting industry.

Above-the-Line: In film, those costs that occur before filming, this includes salaries of the talent and creative team (director, producer, screenwriter), plus any rights required for adapted scripts.

Act: A large division of a full-length play, separated from the other act or acts by an intermission.

Acting Edition: A published play script, typically for use in productions in the amateur market or as reading copies.

Action: The moving pictures we see on screen. Also, the direction given by a director indicating that filming begins.

Actor/Actress: A male or female person who performs a role in a play, work of theatre, or movie.

Act/Scene Heading: Centered, all CAPS heading at the start of an act or scene. Act numbers are written in Roman numerals, scene numbers in ordinals.

Adaptation: The action or process of adapting from a written work, typically a novel, into a movie, television drama, or stage play.

Ad Lib: Dialogue which the characters or actors make up in real time on the movie set or on stage.

Advertising: A technique the writer uses to tell the viewer where the film is going or is the indication of some upcoming experience a character might have.

Aerial Shot: This suggests a shot be taken from a plane/helicopter.

Aftermath: A scene of aftermath follows a dramatically heightened moment (seen or unseen) and allows the characters as well as the audience time to 'digest' the shock, pain, or joy of that moment.

Against: A term describing the ultimate potential payday for a writer in a film deal. $400,000 against $800,000 means that the writer is paid $400,000 when the script is finished (through rewrite and polish); when and if the movie goes into production, the writer gets an additional $400,000.

Agent Submission: A method of submission which a theater requires a script be submitted by a recognized agent.
Alan Smithee: A fictional name taken by a writer or director who doesn't want their real name credited on a film.
Angle: A particular camera placement.
Allegorical Characters: These characters are symbolic, set, and stoney with no possibility of change.
Allegory: A story that sets out to reveal a hidden meaning.
Alienation Effect: Not allow the viewer to suspend their disbelief and get caught up in the world of the play, but make them aware at every turn that they are watching a play.
Alliteration: The repetition of initial identical consonants sounds or vowel sounds (usually at the beginning of a word). Character personalities can sometimes be enhanced with this poetic device.
Angle On: A type of shot. This usually occurs in scenes taking place in large settings.
Antagonist: This character is the protagonist's main adversary.
Anthropomorphic Characters: Flawed but have the possibility of change (a moral transformation or increase in wisdom).
Anthropomorphism: The attribution of human characteristics or behavior to a god, animal, or object.
Antihero: The central character in the script who lacks the conventional heroic attributes.
A Page: A revised page that extends beyond the original page, going onto a second page. (i.e. Page 1, 1A, 2, 3, 3A)
Approved Writer: A writer whom a television network trusts to deliver a good script once hired.
Atmosphere: The impression created by the mood of a setting.
At Rise Description: This is a stage direction at the beginning of an act or scene.
Attached: Agreement by name actors and/or a director to be a part of the making of a movie.
Audience Awareness: How the author wants the audience to be involved. When should something be delayed or revealed?

Audio/Visual Script: A dual column screenplay with video description on the left and audio and dialogue on the right.
b.g.: Abbreviation for "background" (i.e. In the b.g. kids are fighting).
Back Door Pilot: A two-hour TV movie that is a setup for a TV series if ratings warrant further production.
Back End: Payment on a movie project when profits are realized.
Back Story: Experiences of a main character taking place prior to the main action, which contribute to character motivations and reactions.
Bankable: A person who can get a project financed solely by having their name attached.
Beat: A parenthetically noted pause interrupting dialogue, denoted by (beat), for the purpose of indicating a significant shift in the direction of a scene.
Beat Sheet: An abbreviated description of the main events in a screenplay or story.
Bill: The play or plays that constitute what the audience is seeing at any one sitting. Short for "playbill."
Binding: What literally holds the script together, such as brads with card stock covers.
Black Box: A flexible theater space named for its appearance.
Blackout: A common stage direction at the end of a scene or act.
Block Page: A script page that is all action description. Visually, the page is dense, with very little white space, and at looks like a block of paragraphs.
Blocking: The planning and working out of the movements of actors on stage.
Book: The story and the non-musical portion (dialogue, stage directions) of a theatrical musical.
Boom Shot: High-angle shots, typically with the camera moving.
Brads: Brass fasteners used to bind a screenplay printed on three-hole paper.
Bright White Flash To: Whiteness will fill the screen for a brief moment as we pass into the next scene).
Bump: A troublesome element in a script that negatively deflects the reader's attention from the story.

Button: A witty line that "tops off" a scene.
Canted Shot: Tilted 25 to 45 degrees to one side, causing horizontal lines be at an angle.
CARD: Text printed on the screen, either over black or superimposed over an image, that is needed to indicate location, time, date, or era. This written in all CAPS followed by the colon and typed at the same left margin as for character names. Underneath CARD:, the location, era, and date is written at character dialogue margins set off by quotes.
Cast: The characters who are present in the play or film. (double-cast means that the same actor is expected to play both roles).
Cast Page: A page that typically follows the Title Page of a play, listing the characters, with brief descriptions of each.
Catalyst: The event or character that makes the protagonist start to act to fulfill their core dramatic desire.
Catharsis: The emotional release an audience feels after the downfall of a tragic character.
Center Stage: The center of the performance space, used for placement of the actors and the set.
Character: Any personified entity.
Character Arc: The emotional progress of the characters.
Character Core: The character's core personality helps to define who they are, and should be interested and flawed.
Character Description: A few lines of character details when a new character is introduced, so the description will grab the attention of the reader as well as potential actors.
Character Development: The character's looks, background, history, personality, and current goals.
Character Name: When any character speaks, their name appears on the line preceding the dialogue. The name is tabbed to a location that is roughly in the center of the line.
Cheat a Script: Adjusting the margins and spacing of a screenplay on a page to fool the reader into thinking the script is shorter.
Climax: Also called the main culmination, is the ultimate decisive moment at the end of Act Two, in which the character has done everything he or she could do to reach the desired objective, and now he or she faces his/her highest obstacle and the end of the main tension.

Close On: A shot description that strongly suggests a close-up on some object, action, or person.
Closer Angle: The camera moves in nearer to the subject.
Close Up (CU): A very close camera angle on a character or object.
Cold Reading: A reading of a script done by actors who have not previously reviewed the play.
Collaboration: Two or more people working together in a joint intellectual effort.
Commedia dell'arte: A professional form of theatrical improvisation, developed in Italy in the 1500's, featuring stock characters and standardized plots.
Complication: The second act of a three-act dramatic structure, in which "the plot thickens."
Computer Generated Image (CGI): Denoting that computers will be used to generate the full imagery.
Confidant: Usually a minor character, someone the protagonist, or even the antagonist, can confess secrets to, or can tell backstory/exposition to.
Conflict: The heart of drama; someone wants something and people and things keep getting in the way of them achieving it.
Context: This is what influences a character: culture, historical period, location, occupation, etc.
Continuing Dialogue: Dialogue spoken by the same character that continues uninterrupted onto the next page, marked with a (cont'd).
CONTINUOUS: Sometimes, instead of DAY or NIGHT at the end of a Slugline/Location Description, you'll see CONTINUOUS, which refers to action that moves from one location to another without any interruptions in time.
Continuous Action: Stated in the script as CONTINUOUS, and included in the scene heading when moving from one scene to another as the action continues.
Contrast: Two characters that seem to have nothing in common, but with further investigation, it is clear they do.
Contra-Zoom: Also known as the Hitchcock Zoom or the Vertigo Effect, this is an unsettling in-camera special effect that appears to undermine normal visual perception in a way that is difficult to describe.
Copyright: Ownership of an artistic property.

Copyright Notice: Placed on the title page of a script.
Costume: A set of clothes in a style typical of a particular location or historical period. In scripts that take place in present day, costume is not an important element to describe.
Courier 12: The main font and size used for scripts.
Coverage: The notes prepared by readers, typically divided into three sections: plot synopsis, evaluation/discussion of the quality of the writing, and a recommendation that either passes on the script or kicks it on to the next level. Typically, coverage is for internal use and almost never shared with the writer.
Crane Shot: High-angle shots, typically with the camera moving.
Crawl: Superimposed titles or text intended to move across/up/down/diagonally on screen. For example, the text at the beginning of *Star Wars* movies "Crawls" up into infinity.
Critique: Opinions and comments based on predetermined criteria that may be used for self evaluation or the evaluation of the actors or the production itself.
Crossfade: Much like a "Fade to black then Fade to next scene." In other words, as one scene fades out, a moment of black interrupts before the next scene fades in.
Cue: A signal, either verbal or physical, that indicates something else, such as a line of dialogue or an entrance, is about to happen.
Cutaway: A related shot that is "away" from the basic scene. During a basketball game you might "cut away" from the game to a shot of the cheerleaders, the coach, or cheering fans.
Cuts: Instant changes from one scene to the next, as in "Cut to...."
CUT TO: The most simple and common transition. Since this transition is implied by a change of scene, it may be used sparingly to help intensify character changes and emotional shifts. The transition describes a change of scene over the course of one frame.

Delay: A narrative and dramatic device used to strengthen the established tension. The viewer anticipates that certain events will happen, and the tension, hope, and fear grows from that anticipation and creates audience impatience.
Denouement: The final resolution of the conflict in a plot.
Descending Action: At the end of the second act, and after the protagonist has done everything in their power to overcome their supreme ordeal, and the main culmination is reached and the battle is done with either a victory or a defeat, the descending action starts the third act with a new tension.
Designer: Theater professional whose job it is to envision any of the following elements in a play: costumes, sets, lights, sound or properties.
Deus Ex Machina: The thing/angel/magic that swoops in to save the day.
Development: The process of preparing a script for production.
Dialogue: The speeches between characters.
Directing on the Page: Something a screenwriter wants to avoid, when the writer provides too many camera positions such as ZOOM IN, PAN LEFT, ANGLE ON, CRANE SHOT, CLOSE UP, PUSH IN, TRACKING SHOT, etc. If it is important for the screenwriter make the audience aware of a particular prop or object, the writer should find a way to highlight that object without using camera shots.
Direct Solicitation: When a theater contacts a playwright or his agent about submitting a script.
Director: The individual responsible for staging (i.e. placing in the space or "blocking") the actors, sculpting and coordinating their performances, and making sure they fit with the design elements into a coherent vision of the script.
Dissection: An oral or written summary, comments and critiques of the play, often after a public reading.
Dissolves: Two scenes momentarily overlap during a transition from one to the other.
DISSOLVE TO: This is a common transition. As one scene fades out, the next scene fades into place. This type of transition is generally used to convey some passage of time.

Dolly: A mechanism on which a camera can be moved around a scene or location.
Downstage (or Down): The part of the stage closest to the audience, so named because when stages were raked (slanted), an actor walking toward the audience was literally walking down.
Draft: A version of a script. Each draft of rewrites/revisions should be numbered differently.
Dramatic Action: An explanation of what the characters are trying to do.
Dramatic Irony: When the audience learns something that at least one person on screen does not know.
Dramatists Guild of America: The professional organization of playwrights, composers and lyricists.
Dramaturg: A professional within a theatre or opera company that deals mainly with research and development of plays or operas.
Dress Rehearsal: The final few rehearsals just prior to opening night in which the show is run with full technical elements with full costumes and makeup.
Dual Dialog: When two characters speak simultaneously.
Dutch Angle: Shot (on the right) and tilted 25 to 45 degrees to one side, causing horizontal lines be at an angle.
Editing: When a film is pieced together to flow as the director suggests.
Emphasized Dialogue: Dialogue that the playwright wants stressed, usually identified with italics.
Epic Theater: Plays that work with many characters, sets, and that span large amounts of time.
Establishing Shot: A cinematic shot that establishes a certain location or area.
Evening-Length Play: A play that constitutes a full evening of theater on its own (a.k.a. Full-Length Play).
Exposition: The first act of a dramatic structure, in which the main conflict and characters are "exposed" or revealed. Also, any information about the characters, conflict or world of the script.
EXT.: Outdoors.

Extension: A technical note placed directly to the right of the Character name that denotes how the character's voice is heard. For example, O.S. stands for Off-Screen.
Extreme Close-Ups (XCUs): Reserved for dramatic impact. The XCU shot may show just the eyes of an individual.
Extremely Long Shot (XLS): The camera is placed a very long distance from the subject or action. Generally, this term would be left out of a screenplay and left to the director to decide.
f.g.: Abbreviation for "foreground" (i.e. In the f.g., kids are fighting).
FADE IN: Used at the start of a screenplay.
FADE OUT: Used at the end of a screenplay.
Falling Action: The series of events following the climax of a plot.
Favor On: A particular character or action is highlighted or "favored" in a shot. The focus is basically centered on someone or something in particular.
Feature Film: Generally defined as any film at least one hour long and made primarily for distribution in theaters.
Film Festival: A festival of short and/or feature-length films shown over the course of a few days to a few weeks.
First Culmination: The first decisive moment in which the character faces his/her highest obstacle so far. This moment usually parallels the end of the film; therefore, if the film is a tragedy, then the first culmination should be a low point for the character. If the character wins in the end, then the first culmination should be a victory for the character.
Flashback: A scene from the past that interrupts the action to explain motivation or reaction of a character to the immediate scene.
Flash Cut: An extremely brief shot, sometimes as short as one frame, which is nearly subliminal in effect. Also a series of short staccato shots that create a rhythmic effect.
Flash Pan: A quick snap of the camera from one object to another that blurs the frame and is often used as a transition. Cuts are often hidden in swish pans, or they can be used to disorient or shock the audience.

Formula: More commonly used in the world of film than for describing the stage, it usually refers to a "sure-fire" method of structuring a script (i.e. it must include certain elements and arrive at a certain ending).
Freeze Frame: The image on the screen stops, freezes and becomes a still shot.
French Scene: The smaller unit of a Scene containing a slight change in the dynamics on stage any time a character exits or enters.
Freytag's Triangle: Rising action, crisis or climax, perhaps a realization (epiphany), then a falling off or dénouement, and closure which is the classic structure of traditional narrative.
Full-Length Play: Also known as an Evening Length Play, a play that constitutes a full evening of theater.
Full Shot: This is a shot from the top of their heads to at least their feet.
Genre: The category a story or script falls into - such as: thriller, romantic comedy, action, science fiction, etc.
Green Light: A project approved for production.
Handheld Shot: A handheld camera shot that moves in a walking or running motion while following an actor.
Header: An element of a Production Script occupying the same line as the page number, which is on the right and .5" from the top. Printed on every script page, header information includes the date of a revision and the color of the page.
Heat: Positive gossip about a project on the Hollywood grapevine.
High Concept: A brief statement of a movie's basic idea that is felt to have tremendous public appeal.
Hip Pocket: A casual relationship with an established agent in lieu of a signed, formal agreement.
Hitchcock Zoom: The setting of a zoom lens is used to adjust the field of view at the same time as the camera moves towards or away from the subject in such a way as to keep the subject the same size in the frame throughout.
Hook: Describes what catches the public's attention and keeps them interested in the flow of a story.

Horizontal Reading: It is text-heavy, with blocks of description that are more than four lines in length. This results in a slower, more labor-intensive read.

I/E (INT./EXT. or INTERIOR/EXTERIOR): Beginning the slugline, the abbreviation I/E indicates that the scene will take place both inside and outside. I/E scenes often take place inside and outside of moving automobiles. Clearly the car itself is outside as it moves through a particular environment, but the characters are inside the vehicle.

Inciting Incident: Also known as Point of Attack, this is the moment, and first major plot point, at which the dramatic conflict, hidden up until now, announces itself. This moment usually occurs about half way through the first act.

Indie: A production company independent of major film studio financing.

Indirection: When a character sees something he cannot hear or hears something he cannot see, and acts based on this incomplete information.

Insert (or Insert Shot): When a writer pictures a certain close-up at a certain moment in the film, he or she may use an insert shot. This describes a shot of some important detail in a scene that must be given the camera's full attention for a moment. Inserts are mainly used in reference to objects, a clock, or actions, putting a key in a car's ignition. Writing important objects in CAPS will convey their importance in the scene.

INT.: Indoors.

Intercut: A script instruction denoting that the action moves back and forth between two or more scenes.

Intermission: A break between acts or scenes of the play to allow for set changes.

Interrupt: When one character cuts off another's dialogue, sometimes marked with an ... or with an em dash (—).

In the Round: A type of theater space in which the audience is, usually in a circular configuration, on all sides of the playing area.

Into Frame (or Into View): The audience can only see so much through the window of a movie screen. Use this term to suggest something or someone comes into the picture while the camera stays put or a character or object coming from off stage in the theater.

I Page: A script page that is all dialogue. With no action description to break up the page, the visual page looks like a capital 'I' with a column of white space on both the left and right of the page.
Iris Out (or Wipe To or Iris Fade Out or Iris Fade In): A wipe from the center of the frame out in all directions. It's as if the iris of a human eye were opening for dimly lit situations to take us into the next scene or the ending credits.
Jib Shot: High-angle shots, typically with the camera moving.
JUMP CUT TO: A transition which denotes a linkage of shots in a scene in which the appearance of real continuous time has been interrupted by omission. Transitions from one moment to the next within a scene that appear jarring because they break the direct flow of filmic time and space.
LAP DISSOLVE: A transition between scenes that is achieved by fading out one shot while the next one grows clearer.
Lights Fade: A common stage direction to end a scene or an act.
Lights Up: Transition used in Stage format, denoting the beginning and discovery of a scene by the illumination of lights onto a particular area of the stage.
Line Reading: When a director or playwright gives an actor a specific way to perform a line of dialogue.
Literary Manager: The artistic officer of a theater in charge of at least the first stages of reviewing scripts for possible production.
Literary Office: Usually headed by the literary manager and often staffed with interns and in-house or freelance readers. Typically the place to direct script submissions and inquiries.
Location: The particular setting a scene takes place.
Locked Pages: A software term for finalized screenplay pages that are handed out to the department heads and talent for production.
Lock In: At the end of Act One, the main character is "locked-in" the predicament that is central to the story, propelling them into a new direction to obtain their goal.

Logline: A 25 words or less description of a screenplay.
Long Shot (LS): Camera shot that is taken at a considerable distance from the subject, usually containing a large number of background objects. Always spelled out in capital letters.
Lyrics: The words that are sung by characters in a musical.
M.O.S.: Without sound, so described because a German-born director wanting a scene with no sound told the crew to shoot "mit out sound."
Magic (or Magic Hour): The short period of time around sunset.
Manuscript: A script before it has been published.
Manuscript Format: The ideal submission format.
Master Scene Script: A script formatted without scene numbering (the usual format for a spec screenplay).
Match Cut: A transition in which something in the scene that follows in some way directly matches a character or object in the previous scene.
Main Culmination (or Climax): The ultimate decisive moment at the end of Act Two, where the character has done everything they could do to reach the desired objective, and now they face their highest obstacle and the end of the main tension.
Major Dramatic Question (MDQ): The main premise or theme of the play.
Master Shot: Similar to an establishing shot, but this term is generally reserved for the special needs of film. Once master shot action is filmed the scene is generally shot over again from different camera positions so that there are shots (especially close-ups) of each actor. Dialogue, and actor reactions and movements are repeated each time the camera is repositioned.
MATCH DISSOLVE TO: This contains similar qualities to the MATCH CUT. A match dissolve involves two objects of similar color, shape, and/or movement in transition from one scene to the next.
Montage: In film, this is a series of images showing a theme, a contradiction, or the passage of time.
Medium Close-Up (MCU): A shot cropped between the shoulders and the belt line.

Medium Shot (MS): Camera shot often used to describe a shot of character approximately from the waist up.

Midpoint (or First Culmination): The first decisive moment where the character faces their highest obstacle so far.

Midpoint Contract: The first culmination (or midpoint) and the main culmination (end of act two) are almost always in contrast with each other.

Midpoint Mirror: The first culmination (or midpoint) and the end of the film usually mirror each other. If the protagonist wins in the end of the script, then he should have a victory at the midpoint. If it's a tragic ending for our hero, then he should also have a tragedy at the midpoint.

Miniseries: A long-form movie of three hours or more shown on successive nights or weeks.

Monologue: A long speech by one character, usually preaching or lecturing to others when the conflict is at a high point.

Montage: A cinematic device used to show a series of scenes, all related and building to some conclusion.

Mood: The atmosphere or pervading tone of the scene, sequence, act, or even the entire script.

Moving (or Moving Shot): Camera shot which follows whatever is being filmed.

Multiple Casting: When an actor plays more than one character.

Musical: A play in which songs and music are an integral part of the dramatic structure.

Musical Numbers Page: A page in a musical script, usually following the Cast Page, that lists the musical numbers, divided by act, and the characters that sing in them.

Next Scene: The end of a major movement in the film. This is often days, months, or years after the previous scenes. Sometimes titles will appear in the blackness to declare a passage of time. But this transition is often a sign of a major shift in time or emotional status for the main characters. It may also be used to suggest a character has been knocked out or killed.

Notes: Ideas about a screenplay shared with a screenwriter by someone responsible for moving the script forward into production, which the screenwriter is generally expected to use to revise the script. A similar paradigm exists on stage, with notes coming most often from the dramaturg or director.
Numbered Scenes: Numbers that appear to the right and left of the scene heading to aid the Assistant Director in breaking down the scenes for scheduling and production.
O.C.: Abbreviation for Off Camera, denoting that the speaker is resident within the scene but not seen by the camera.
O.S.: Abbreviation for Off Screen, denoting that the speaker is not resident within the scene.
Obligatory Scene: A scene which the viewer usually expects and looks forward to.
Obstacles: Conflicts that occur throughout the entire script.
Off: Short for offstage. Typically written as (off) next to a character name when a character speaking dialogue is offstage while she speaks.
One-Act Play: Technically, a play that has only one act, but in more common usage, a play that is not an evening unto itself but instead usually runs no more than an hour. A common arrangement is to produce three half-hour long one-acts on the same bill.
One-Hour Episodic: A screenplay for a television show whose episodes fill a one-hour time slot, week to week.
One-String Characters: Usually appear in one or just a few scenes and have primarily only a functional role belonging to a location, place, or environment. They do not suggest any special story line of their own nor are they involved in any dramatic predicament, and therefore, if they reappear in the story again, they repeat the same 'one-string' effect.
Opening Credits: Onscreen text describing the most important people involved in the making of a movie.
Option: The securing of the rights to a screenplay for a given length of time.
Package: The assembly of the basic elements necessary to secure financing for a film.

Pan: A camera direction indicating a stationary camera that pivots back and forth or up and down.

Parenthetical: Also known as a "wryly" because of the propensity of amateur screenwriters to try to accent a character's speech -- as in BOB (wryly) -- an inflection to a speech noted by a writer. Of course, in stageplays, all stage directions (at least in Manuscript Format) are in parentheses, but "directing off the page," as it's often called, is equally frowned upon.

Persona: A specific and cohesive voice or personality.

Pitch: To verbally describe a property to a potential buyer in the hope it will be bought.

Planting and Payoff: A device by which a motif, a line of dialogue, a gesture, behavioral mannerism, costume, prop or any combination of these is introduced into a story and then repeated as the story progresses. In the changed circumstances toward the resolution, the planted information assumes a new meaning and "pays off."

Play: Sometimes known as a stageplay, it's a production meant to be performed on stage in front of a live audience.

Playwright: A person who writes stage plays.

Playwriting: The craft or act of writing scripts for the stage.

Plot: The main events of the story, devised by the writer, and presented as an interrelated whole. In a screenplay the plot is structured through three acts, including eight main sequences (sometimes nine or ten), and five major plot points.

Point of Attack (or Inciting Incident): This is the moment, and first major plot point, where the dramatic conflict, hidden up until now, announces itself. This moment occurs about half way through the first act.

Points: Percentage participation in the profits of a film.

Polish: In theory, to rewrite a few scenes in a script to improve them. In practice, a screenwriter is often expected to do a complete rewrite of a script for the price of a polish.

POV: Point of View; a camera angle placed so as to seem the camera is the eyes of a character.

Premise: The theme of the play.

Presentational: A play in which the audience is recognize as an audience and the play as a play; consequently the actors may speak directly to the audience.

Producer: The person or entity financially responsible for a stage or film production.

Production Script: A script in which no more major changes or rewrites is anticipated to occur, which is used day by day for filming on a movie set.

Professional Recommendation: A method of submission where a writer submits a full script if it's accompanied by a theater professional (typically a literary manager or artistic director.

Prop: An item (e.g. gun, spoon, brush, etc.) that is held by one of the characters or in the scene or on stage.

Property: Any intellectual property in any form (including a play or screenplay) that might form the basis of a movie.

Proscenium: A type of stage in which the actors play opposite the audience, from which they are separated.

Protagonist: The leading character in the script. They are usually depicted as the hero. Occasionally the protagonist is an antihero.

Published Play Format: Meant to save space, the character names are on the left and stage directions occur on the same lines as dialogue.

Pull Back: The camera physically moves away from a subject, usually through a zoom or dolly action.

Pull Focus: The camera focus changes from one object or subject to another.

Push In: The camera physically moves towards a subject.

Query: A method of submission in which a writer approaches a theater with a brief letter, sometimes accompanied by a synopsis and sample pages.

Quid Pro Quo: When a character or the audience mistakes someone or something for someone or something else.

Raissoneur: Usually a supporting character who helps the audience keep track of the values of the story.

Rake: A stage that is slanted so that as an actor moves away from the audience, he gets higher. It's more likely now that the audience be raked.

Reader (or Script Reader): A person who reads screenplays for a production company.

Reading: A "performance" of a play in which the actors are script-in-hand. It could either take place around a table (called a "table reading") or with some blocking or staging (a "staged reading").
Recognition: When a character finds out what the audience already knows.
Register of Copyrights: The US government office that registers intellectual property (e.g. scripts), necessary prior to filing a claim for copyright infringement in court.
Release: A legal document given to unrepresented writers for signing by agents, producers or production companies, absolving said entities of legal liability.
Resolution: The third act of a dramatic structure, in which the conflict comes to some kind of conclusion: the protagonist either gets it or doesn't.
Reversal: A place in the plot where a character achieves the opposite of his aim, resulting in a change from good fortune to bad fortune.
Reestablishing Shots: Reminders or updates on scene changes where people have moved.
Relevance Test: When building characters, ask if the element of a character's history affects the character's actions during the onstage course of the story.
Representational: A play performed as if the audience as if the audience is watching the action through an imaginary fourth wall.
Reverse Angle: The script suggests the camera come around 180 degrees to get a shot from the "other side" of a scene.
Revised Pages: Changes are made to the script after the initial circulation of the Production Script, which are different in color and incorporated into the script without displacing or rearranging the original, unrevised pages.
Rhythm: Each scene and each sequence has its own rhythm, its pulse, its tempo, its pacing.
Rising Action: When a dramatic situation that contains a serious conflict has been created, rising action begins and continues to build until the character finds a way to solve the conflict.
Romcom: A comedic movie that revolves around a romance.

Run-Through: A rehearsal moving from start to finish without stopping for corrections or notes.
Scene: Action taking place in one location and in a distinct time that moves the story to the next element of the story.
Scene Heading (or Slugline): A short description of the location and time of day of a scene. For example: EXT. CABIN - DAY.
Scenes of Preparation: Scenes of a character getting ready for the dramatic confrontation ahead.
Screening: The showing of a film for test audiences and/or people involved in the making of the movie.
Screenwriter: The screenwriter writes the script that provides the foundation for the film or stageplay.
Screenwriting: The art of writing scripts for a visual medium.
Script: The document that outlines a movie or stageplay through visual descriptions, actions of characters and their dialogue.
Script Cover: What protects the script on its travels between the writer and its many potential readers.
Script Writing Software: Computer software designed specifically to format and aid in the writing of screenplays and teleplays.
Sequences: Thematic units of action, each one usually between 10 to 15 minutes that has its own specific tension and an event around which it is focussed.
Set: The physical elements that are constructed or arranged to create a sense of place.
Setting: The time and place of a play or screenplay.
SFX (or SPFX): Abbreviation for Sound Effects.
Shooting Script: A script that has been prepared for production.
Shot: What the camera sees. For example, TRACKING SHOT would mean that the camera is following a character or character as he walks in a scene. WIDE SHOT would mean that we see every character that appears in the scene, all at once.
Showrunner: A writer/producer ultimately responsible for the production of a TV series, week to week.
Simultaneous Dialogue: When two characters speak at the same time, written in two columns side by side.

Sitcom: A 30-minute comedic TV show revolving around situations the characters repeatedly fall into.
Slugline: Another name for the Scene Heading.
Smash Cut: A quick or sudden cut from one scene to another.
Soap Opera: Daytime dramas that were originally sponsored by the makers of laundry detergent.
Soliloquy: A speech spoken by a character alone on stage that reveals the character's innermost thoughts to the audience.
Spec Script: A script written without being commissioned on the speculative hope that it is sold.
Split Screen: A screen with different scenes taking place in two or more sections; the scenes are usually interactive, as in the depiction of two sides of a phone conversation.
Stage Center: More commonly known as Center Stage, it is the center of the performance space.
Stage Directions: In a stageplay, the instructions in the text for the actors (e.g. entrances, exit, significant actions or business) and stage crew (e.g. lights fade). Also, in a musical, the person who directed the non-musical elements of the show may be credited with "Stage Direction" to distinguish him from the Music Director, who will be credited with "Music Direction."
Stage Left: On stage, the actors' left, assuming they are facing the audience. "Left" for short.
Stage Right: On stage, the actors' right, assuming they are facing the audience. "Right" for short.
Status Quo: The existing state of affairs of the main character daily life and his/her world.
Steadicam: A camera built to remain stable while being moved, usually by human hands.
Stereotypical Characters: An oversimplified image or idea of a particular type of person or thing.
Stock Footage: Footage of events in history from other films and/or television broadcasts.
Stock Shot: A sequence of film previously shot and available for purchase and use from a film library.
Storyboards: Illustrations or images that are organized and displayed in a sequence for the purpose of pre-visualizing a film, animation, or interactive media.

Style: The distinctive and unique manner in which a writer arranges words to achieve particular effects.

Subjective Shot: The audience (camera) will see what the character sees.

Submission: A script that is submitted to producers or agents.

Subplot Characters: These characters either help, initiate, complicate, or fight the hero's efforts.

Subtext: What the character is really saying between the lines, and it is revealed by character's actions and reactions.

Suggested Setting: A setting where a few set pieces take the place of elaborate set construction.

SUPERIMPOSE (or SUPER): The laying one image on top of another, usually words over a filmed scene, always typed in CAPS.

Swish Pan (also Pan): Camera movement involving the camera turning on a stationary axis.

Symbolic Characters: One-dimensional, usually personifying only one quality or idea, such as love, wisdom, mercy, or justice.

Synopsis: A two to three page, double-spaced description of a screenplay.

Tag: A short scene at the end of a movie that usually provides some upbeat addition to the climax.

Technical Demands: The extent to which a play requires specific lighting, sound, sets, etc.

Ten-Minute Play: A complete play, with a beginning, middle and end, designed to play in ten minutes.

The Business: Show business in general.

Theatre of the Absurd: Theatrical movement beginning in the 1950s in which playwrights created works representing the universe as unknowable and humankind's existence as meaningless.

Three Shot: Designate shots of two or three people in one scene.

The Third Act Twist: A surprising, yet explainable and motivated change in the direction of the action of the overall story line and new third act tension. This moment occurs at the end of the seventh sequence in the middle of the third act.

Thriller: A fast-paced, high stakes crime story in which the protagonist is generally in danger at every turn, with the most danger coming in the final confrontation with the antagonist.
Thrust: A stage configuration in which the playing area protrudes into the audience; the actors have audience on three sides of them.
Tight On: A close-up of a person or thing that is used for dramatic effect.
TIME CUT: When you want to cut to later in a scene, you have the option of writing TIME CUT as the transition.
Title Page: A page of the script that contains the title and the author's contact information.
Topical Reference: A brand name or a dated trendy detail that may not be understood by all audiences later.
Touring Play: A play with minimal technical demands that is meant to be easily packed up and moved from one performance space to another.
Tracking Shot (or Track, Tracking, Travelling): A tracking shot involves a camera following a person or an object. As long as the camera isn't locked down in place by a tripod, for example, and is following (tracking) a subject, then it's a tracking shot.
Tragedy: Used as a noun, the stage area away from the audience. As a verb, to steal the focus of a scene.
Trailer: A theatrical advertisement for an upcoming film attraction.
Transition: A script notation denoting an editing transition within the telling of a story. For example, DISSOLVE TO: means the action blurs and refocuses into another scene, and is generally used to denote a passage of time.
Treatment: A scene by scene description of a screenplay, minus all or most of the dialogue.
Truck: When a lateral move is needed.
Twist (or Reversal): A surprising, yet explainable and motivated change in the direction of the action, either within a scene, a sequence, or in the overall story line.
Two Shot: Camera shot of two people, usually from the waist up.
Unity of Action: The cohesiveness that brings all the elements: conflict, crisis, characters, and action together.

Unsolicited Script: A method of script submission in which the writer sends the script, without prior contact, to the theater or production company.

Upstage: The part of the stage farthest from the audience, so named because when stages were raked (slanted), an actor walking away from the audience was literally walking up. Called "Up" for short.

V.O.: Abbreviation for Voice Over, denoting that the speaker is narrating the action onscreen.

Vertical Reading: Scripts that have a lot of white space, which helps the reader to skim quickly, shot by shot, and see the film as the writer envisioned it.

Visuals: Revealing information bit by bit by showing, not telling the audience.

White Space: The more white space the page has, the more vertical it becomes, making it a faster read. White space breaks up action into smaller sections as well as allows the story to be delivered shot by shot.

WIDE SHOT: Camera shot that is taken at a considerable distance from the subject, usually containing a large number of background objects. Always spelled out in capital letters.

Wipe To: A transition in which one scene "wipes away" for the next. Imagine Scene A is water and Scene B is the substance underneath. A wipe would look like a squeegee pulling Scene A off of Scene B. These usually suggest a passage of time from one scene to the next.

Workshop: A developmental "production" of a play, with a significant amount of rehearsal, but with less fully realized production values (e.g. set) than a full production.

Writers Guild of America (or WGA): The main organization for screenwriters in the US.

Zoom: The image seems to close in on a person or object making the person or object appear larger (or smaller) on screen. Notice and recognize the difference between a zoom and a push in (camera moves closer to subject).

Printed in Great Britain
by Amazon